And Then
There Was Rain

And Then There Was Rain

Kristin Baker

iUniverse LLC
Bloomington

AND THEN THERE WAS RAIN

iUniverse books may be ordered through booksellers or by contacting:

iUniverse LLC
1663 Liberty Drive
Bloomington, IN 47403
www.iuniverse.com
1-800-Authors (1-800-288-4677)

Because of the dynamic nature of the Internet, any web addresses or links contained in this book may have changed since publication and may no longer be valid. The views expressed in this work are solely those of the author and do not necessarily reflect the views of the publisher, and the publisher hereby disclaims any responsibility for them.

Any people depicted in stock imagery provided by Thinkstock are models, and such images are being used for illustrative purposes only. Certain stock imagery © Thinkstock.

ISBN: 978-1-4917-2608-2 (sc)
ISBN: 978-1-4917-2609-9 (e)

Library of Congress Control Number: 2014903138

Printed in the United States of America.

iUniverse rev. date: 03/06/2014

Table of Contents

1. The Art of Being Cold

Trust is a very important thing to me.
yet it's something
I've never earned
nor ever learned to possess.

I Can't Feel My Heart

I can't feel my heart.
but I knew exactly how it felt
to cry in the shower
so no one would hear me;
what it was like
to wait for everyone
to have fallen asleep
and stay up all night,
peering at the stars left outside
hoping for answers
to settle my strife.
And when I
found myself
begging for
someone else's life
to be just a little more
significant than mine
so I wouldn't
feel as bad
about hating them.
I knew how it felt
to have my heart
ripped from my soul
over someone
I'd never met,
never seen,

never known;
and still had known
everything I thought they were.
I knew what it was like
to train my body
to be immune to hurt
or feelings for anything
that could leave me alone,
in the dark.
Because I knew
disappointment.
I knew what it felt like
to have no sense of change
because false hopes had left me
exhausted and drained.
I don't know what it's like
to be absolutely
sure about anything.
To know the difference
between right and wrong,
dead or living,
truth or lies,
real or faking.
I don't know what love
is supposed to be.
What is worse,
is that no one
seemed to ever know
when I was telling the truth

Kristin Baker

or when I was
faking a smile
in the presence
of bittersweet freedom.
I can't feel my heart anymore,
but I knew how it felt.

Gray & Bored

If you do not see her when you walk,
you do not know.
She is not the essence of good,
but of nothing.
She is not sweet like the sunny rays
that shine through the clouds,
nor as loud as the silent pin
in the cold, rigid crowd.
And when you see
her boring into you, and hesitating,
you might need to worry,
for she sees who you are.
Her face is blank and pale
and pure and honest
and cold as blood that trembles.
You do not see her-
she is hardly even there.
Deep-set eyes and open-
naked for ones that
think they can see.
She is not good,
but nothing of nothing.
And she opens you up
with her gray, bored eyes.
Deep-set gray,
hard, honest bored.
And the things you cannot see . . .

Mr. Sun

Mr. Sun was given the gift of sight.

When he gazed upon God's first creation,

he found white dots, black dots, and brown dots,

and he made red dots.

Mr. Sun never knew these dots were people;

Mr. Sun was never given the gift of knowing.

So he killed the dots.

Mr. Sun was given the gift of life and death.

And the brown dots died,

and the black dots died,

and the white dots died.

But he looked over all that he had done,

and he asked God to bring them back.

So God gave them life.

And Mr. Sun no longer had the gift

of life and death.

Imprisoned

Upward gazes the curious meadow bird,
wishing she could leave her prison in the bay
and join those silver hawks, exploring the world,
as they glide and wave past her today.

The silver hawks do not understand,
teasing and taunting the bird who cannot fly.
Oh, poor creature, imprisoned by the land
and the pain inflicted from Satan's lies.

Legend of Rain

The Arizona rain scatters fast across the desert
stomping like the feet of marching soldiers at war.
The scent is its own reward; the dry eroded soil
is called into a conversion of the elements,
reducing the remains of foliage into an indomitable perfume
greater than the sweetest spice created from earth and sky together
so that not one can turn away from its mark of nature.
Your shout gets swallowed by the heavy clapping of thunder,
calling to one another in battle, but monstrously drowned out.
You can pound at the air as hard as you want,
but you'll never make the hurdling cracking bend to your mortal will.
You'll never hit it with your feeble, forcing hands.
It has its own intermittent destiny, to carry out the falling daggers,
skipping up and down your skin as an enthusiastic pianist.
The strike of lightning is all there is to show off the sleet.
Those daggers sting, pricking memories of salty warm tears.
It is something to be appreciated, but more than that.
It's as if it enraptures you with the power of all the senses brought in together.
No, not even man's forcing hand can hold back
the inevitable fury of nature.
And not even darkness itself can hide from nature
throwing its bolts of pure vitality.
All the dark is allowed to do is shrink down
to a hardened gray shadow at our feet.
Given the gift of rain, God grants us a sense of wisdom-
one we'd never know about were it not the grace
of the gale's mighty hand to begin with.
The shades of a bleak gray haze are all that remain on the earth of the encounter.

The Life You Could Have Had

The winter has fallen
and the knees of the fallen
down onto silvering emeralds.
Merciless death is growing
in cages of thorn twigs
and grotesque cavern minds.
One's death, though as swift as a spirit to touch us
or heartfelt as a pointed sword,
is sweeter when life was contented with misery-
that is to say,
why must we change?
In an aftermath we face
what all is conjured up;
the idea that we fight for
is our hope of what lies beyond.
Our hearts ignore our instincts
and trouble our minds with their own
corrupt, satanic emotions.
You hide yourself in moments
that seem to stop time.
All there was is what the light of love touches.
It is not strong enough to withstand
the burnt summer tassels that fare how we
procure innocence and strife.
We know nothing regarding these secrets,
so the untold catches my breath,
makes me wonder and feel
and die for once. Our pain kills the
other roots we spread in the grave.

Any profound chain of memories
loses us what might have been.
Its doubt is like a sword,
and strikes down hell's demons.
Possessed in them, we feed as tassels,
the hate, the cold, the fall,
then the life you could have had,
and the promise summer had kept
was lost in the coming of winter.

13 Haikus (Wherever I Go)

Wherever I go
I am always moving on
as a bird drifting.

Places call me near.
There are no ties binding me.
They ask me to stay.

My name means little
and to me it is a curse
passing my dream by.

My dream to be known
as someone that I am not,
higher than the trees.

With their arms grasping,
they fall with the heave of leaves.
Many to surpass.

Leaves will surpass me,
in numbers they gather strength
'til the fall winds reach.

They fight off evil
and we see ourselves no more.
Victory has stung.

We live the same lives,
acting as though we're patient
as demons stalk us.

But there is still hope
rising up against our loss,
a hope that searches.

It lurks in our hearts,
a move guiding our journey,
a light as a bond.

It loves us in fear.
It will wipe away our tears.
It fights our great way.

Before the ties break,
our flight invokes stormy clouds.
I keep on running.

'Til I find refuge.
This fear traps me to the earth.
Tears fog up my eyes.

If Thunder Could Speak

If thunder could speak, would you hear the voice of God?
Would you tremble, seeing his face of imaginary colors,
then turn to darkness?
If sins were physical, if you burned them,
would it sound like the demons of hell, screeching in your ears?
Would it look like a smoky purple-black screen?
Would it be poisoned so you cannot even be in its presence?
Would it be so blinding-bright you couldn't see into it?
If rain could curve, would it be like a hand around your face?
Could it caress you like velvety fabric?
Would it feel as warm as a sunny day?
If tears were rain, would they fall from the sky,
landing lightly on your eyes, and trickle down your face
and disguise your tears?
If lightning could follow thunder, would the shock be painful?
Would you cry tears of rain?
If flames were toxic and black, could you taste them
without choking up, and tears fogging?
If thunder could speak, would you fear for death?

Dream World

In Dream World,
everything happens all at once
and not on our time.
In Dream World
I am beautiful,
like a princess who does nothing wrong.
I drift around on a cloud
of innocence and fun.
The faces of people I see have names
but are changed in some way in my imagination.
In Dream World,
I do whatever comes to me,
and nothing is impossible.
I am not scared that I've never
done it before because it's crazy.
In Dream World
I can be anyone,
I can be anywhere,
whether I love the new places
or fear them.
I can be who I've always wanted to be,
living a different life.
In Dream World,
time moves too fast
to hold on to my mistakes.
Emotions control what I do,
even if they don't make any sense,
and I am immortal.

School Bells

For my little brother

School bells chime.
The ring of a clock.
We march in a line
straight forward as a moving snake.
Behind me and in front,
my friends, those I couldn't
go somewhere without.
Before another chime has rung,
to music class we march.

Kindergarten, my favorite year.
I sat near those, my friends once more.
As the others sing, we huddle laughing,
noisy children, adding to the sounds of music.
Miss Renkley- we called her Miss Wrinkly-
she taught us not to sing.
That, or we never listened.
Before the school bells rang
we march in a line;
straight forward as a moving snake.
To gym class we march.

we cannot feel any pain
as we fall 'til we bleed,
as we run 'til we can't breathe,
as we knock each other down,
my friends and I,
only us together.
I called one Logan,
the tall one, the smart one.
I called my best friend Alex,
the troublemaker, the clown;
he may has well have had a red glowing nose.
And 'til the last school bell slowly chimed,
straight forward in a line
as a moving snake we marched
to the class we only wrote in.

I Am No Star

I am no star.
I answer to no one.
A star is a leader.
It takes responsibility,
filling the twilight
with optimistic joy,
love and sweetness.
I am no star.
I scowl up to heaven,
dreading the coming morning
and hiding, unwilling to be stirred
from my lonely black hole.
I swore to raise no shade,
to persuade others
to join me here.
Yet I find it difficult
to stay here so alone
and unable to be stirred

from this pit   of nothing
and watch   all the stars
acting so   sorrowful.
I don't desire   their pity.
I wish to be   no star.
I wish to be   in shade,
in the protection   of the trees.
They fall on me,   covering me,
branches cut me,   reminding me . . .

No Star

I am no star,
healthy and alive- a purpose in the infinite sky,
a star that is bright, buzzing, or electric blue.
My stars trick their victims,
believing lies as measurable followers.
I scowl at a chance to be consoled,
and light will hide my shame and fear.
But darkness shows
how I am troubled by my failures
of playing with risks of those around me.
I am not strong enough to fend off my demons,
and my fears won't allow me relief.
Yet these stars are bright,
fearless leaders who protect their pack
and accept responsibility.
I am no star.
My followers would stalk them
and crush them into dust.
They want to laugh with uncontrollable gladness
and lean into the one they love,
and sigh their names with
bright passion and possession.
They gather in clusters
without awaiting the day
that their light goes out,
for they gather too closely for darkness.
I am not that star;
silent curses in my head linger.
Exhaustion unbalances my limbs from carrying weight,

and I wish to cry for days without ceasing,

and to pray for some kind of acceptance,

wishing for Satan to be cast out.

Only does my Lord know full well how vastly I pray.

My heart is pulsing with salty tears

that sting my heart like angry hornets,

as I fall short of the light I am unaware of,

that grows inside me.

I pray wearily

that I shall not be a star.

I am no star.

Kristin Baker

Once, Too Many

For too many times, loving a song
or a book or a place could make you
grow tired of appreciating the simplicity.
Trying something new is an experience
that never grows old.
I painted too many walls,
and they're all different colors.
I fight with too many people,
I win and I lose.
And even winning can seem like a loss.
I watch the clouds roll over,
yet each time they carry with them
unique pictures that constantly change.
I grow older, and change happens to things
I see differently.
Too many times have I held a pen
and started a story I have never seen before.
Too many times have I
stepped outside on a summer midnight,
and watch the moonlight
glisten off soft blades of crisp, bending green grass,
laying my body on it, and staying up all night,
and then sleeping in the day until I sunburn,
and it will still be silent
on the bed of pungent leaves,
until all I feel is grass forever.

Guessing Wrong

Don't let them see you're struggling.
Don't let them tell you're hurting.
Don't let them see the fear.
Don't let them know you're tired.
Don't let them guess the end.
Don't let them lead your way.
Don't show that you're down.
Don't be there when you're not.
Don't listen to their words,
but feel them wholly in your heart.
Don't fear what you don't know.
Don't grasp at mere thin air.
There's nothing you can say
that will make them care.
Don't try to change them.
Don't try to change.
Don't fall or feel.
Don't listen as it whispers.
Don't stand above the trees.
Don't carry their weight.
Don't show that you are finished,
or let them see you at your best.
But make your worst a mightier sword
than any weight they carry.
They know not what it's like to see nothing.
For if you speak,

then where is the magic of them guessing wrong?
And if you speak,
then how will you know you're not wrong?
And lastly, before you go speaking:
don't let them know you're dead.

Hidden

I just wanted to know this isn't my fault,
and I didn't cause this hurt for all these people;
whether it is the days I spend
frozen in place like a statue,
if I really hear those voices telling me,
or it's just what I really want to do.
I can't handle thinking this is my burden.
I couldn't say what I did wrong.
Could I someday have the ability
to break off the pieces I don't want others to see?
I just want to be justified in my lies
and never bothered by my past again.
Is that craving so bad?
I'd rather not see the colors of the world,
or feel the wind caressing me
on a golden, sunny day.
If it means I can never die,
I won't miss those I didn't really know.
For I need a place to myself.
And let me drift back into that zone
I cannot even find in my memories.
Whether it was real as the restless wind
or the suffocating grip of the sun,
or maybe a place I have of my own,
property I can extinguish the sun in,
and a place I can call the shots in.
It is a place for just a child,
to make a dream to live in.
In this place I am faultless.

Never Seen a Star

It may seem sad to know,
but I have never seen a single star.
Yet blindness brings me sight
for what have I seen instead
of a lonesome, cold star?
I see clouds,
and clouds bring the rain,
and rain summons up
the restless pitch of thunder-
for always beats the sound,
calls bright lightning
drawn across my night sky
like strings more delicate
than that in a harsh hand.
Darkness was mistook for
a root in evil acts,
but the true darkness
has never been seen,
because we are blind,
though we see.
This false darkness
hasn't lived up to its name.
We see much in our dark:
I see clouds;
they light up
and drag me in
with shaking whispered voices,
and they see stars-
those lonesome,
white-cold fires.

The Angel

Here is this angel
in my head.
Instead of protecting me,
he gets me to make mistakes.
He whispers words to me
that only I hear.
He makes me look ugly.
He makes me think bad things.
He makes me cheat.
He praises me for lying.
Oh, how he loves to hate me,
and hold me back from succeeding,
to make me feel much too slow.
He blinds me from right,
truth, love, and happiness.
He kills all those near me
so no one else has me.
He makes me cold;
it is how I know he is here.
So cold, so cold, so scared.
I cannot sleep.
I do not eat.
I keep making
these same mistakes
that makes me into
this that I am not,
this that I am becoming.
He laughs at me
because no one knows.

And I too am glad
that they don't see-
for why would I want to change?
He's made me hate change.
and I am late,
and wrong,
and nowhere,
seeing this angel.
Perhaps he is not
an angel at all.

Happy

For my dad

Underneath this face,
besides this song,
away from this game
we play-
not listening to those
voices saying what we
already know;
this warning saying
to be careful,
then avoiding it all,
walking away at the lowest point.
I can't stay-
it isn't a lie.
Don't think about it.
Everything will turn up.
And your name shows
that we didn't even know
what we'd started.
I should've known
I was never happy.
Walk away tonight.

Loveless Child

You know that scream-at-the-top-of-your-lungs-
with-a-smile-that-says-I-need-you-or-ill-die-
feeling that you get when you are sure you have
the most perfect person in your arms?
I don't have that feeling yet.
You know that gut-wrenching-scream-out-with-so-much-pain-
that-you-break-the-blood-vessels-in-your-eyes-and-cry-yourself-
to-sleep-at-night- feeling because you've suddenly realized
you're still alone and your confidence has left you
but you have to hide from the world or
they'll find out you're losing your mind?
I know that feeling.

It's hard to love.
It's hard to live.
It's hard to laugh.
And it's hard to forgive . . .
It's hard to hate.
It's hard to leave.
It's hard to consider.
It's hard to believe . . .
It's hard to look at something you want but don't have.
It's hard to smile when you are breaking down inside.
It's hard to comfort someone else, when you don't
believe in your own words.
It's hard to avoid fear when fear stalks you in your shadows.
It's hard to get close to anyone when everyone
who ever said they'd be there left.
It's hard to do the wrong thing when your

conscience is screaming at you.
It's hard to tell people you've given up,
when they look at you and you look fine.
It's hard to keep from laughing when you know
someone who has the God-given ability to make you smile
in your most depressed moment.
It's hard to look someone in the eye and tell them it's okay,
when it's so obvious to anyone it's not.
It's so hard when inside, you're just dying to not care
about anything anymore, when there is someone you know
whom you could never bear to let down.
It's so hard to not tell someone
everything, when you're this vulnerable and just dying
for anyone's acceptance and understanding . . .

Throughout my life, I was forced to care.
I was forced to love. They never asked for love.
They never tried to get me there slowly. They made me need them.
They questioned every time I didn't speak,
every time I couldn't talk.
They believed everything they thought of me.
They wanted me happy all the time.
Now look at me. Now they know nothing about me.
Now they are somehow confused every time I tell
them something they have never heard me say before.
Now I am a stranger to them, and they still don't know it yet.
Now I have never learned to care.
Now it's exhausting to make myself force a smile.
Now, I'm done worrying about things that don't matter.
Now I have taught myself not to love
anything anymore . . .

Kristin Baker

Why (The art of being cold)

Why didn't anybody ever tell me
there was more to this life than just happiness?
How come I had to figure it out on my own?
Were they just protecting me?
They didn't want me to be scared this early on?
Well, I guess I should say thanks . . .
Or better yet- thanks for caring too much.
Thank you for letting me fall;
a naïve child with no place in the world.
Thanks for making me feel like I am alone,
someone they think is high above the rest.
It is a lie, and it wasn't my fault.
But it is now . . .

An Endless Night

How is it
that in just a short amount of time,
you have just shriveled up
and died inside and outside,
but only in your mind?
Why do we try to be numb,
but never numb enough?
Somehow, the emotions slither back in
through some leaking hole.
How can it be that such a tiny, invisible crack,
in the matter of seconds,
explodes from the pressure
into one hundred thousand giant,
bloodstained pieces?

Why do we want stereotypes
to suddenly be a bad thing?
Didn't we want to be left alone?
Or was it something different?
Did we really long for a certain set of arms
to cradle and protect us
from the vile and nasty things
we see, hear, and feel.
Even if we only just had one second?
Isn't one second of numbness worth the wait?
Or did we just wait so long,
the crack couldn't hold itself
together anymore, and out of nowhere,
couldn't wait a second longer?

So that when you got here,
it would be too late.

Why are you always
just a little too late?
Where were you?
Why do we ask questions
we already know the answers to?
Maybe, we are afraid of the answer.
Maybe we are afraid of everything,
and your absence shattered
the leaking wound, almost before it could
miraculously heal.
Where is this wound?
How could something so painful,
it brings you to tears
have originated from your mind?
Or perhaps we may just not want
the answer we already know.
So give us another!

Is the wound in our hearts?
How? We have sealed our hearts
to prevent any future complications.
Our hearts are numb;
we have made them that way.
There are no hearts!

Is the wound, then, in our feet?
Are we tired of walking,
of just moving on instead of dealing
with the problem?
Are we so lost that our feet
can't take anymore and want a rest?
But we haven't walked, not really.
Have we been secretly holding on to the problem?
Where are we now?
We haven't changed.

Then could the wound be in our eyes?
Are we tired of searching for a light?
We have given up long ago.
This darkness we chose,
can now hold our secrets,
our problems, our fears, and comfort us.
It is quiet here.
No one is expecting us now.
It is peaceful here.
Death would be a pleasure here, a lifeline.
But we are still alive,
so our eyes aren't the last problem.

Is the wound our thoughts and actions?
We have lost our minds now.
Can they really feel pain?
Our dark thoughts are clouded and confused.
So why do we think we know what is wrong,
when we clearly don't?
There is no hope.

Kristin Baker

For why would we be searching for it
in an endless night?

But, may our answer be everything.
Maybe we aren't as strong
as we thought and the pain is slipping
silently into our hearts.
Maybe we refuse to walk
because we fear change.
Maybe we are blind.
Maybe we are crazy and incoherent,
unresponsive to our lack of action.
And with all of this, the pain lies deeper,
deep into the toxic black
smoky fire which lies to us.
Us, we me and all the rest-
for I am not the only one,
yet I am still alone.
Others care and love me,
but I feel either a sad, empty,
wrenching feeling,
or a terrified, lonely feeling.
What do they love about me?
What do they see that I don't?
I cannot go anywhere,
and this awkward sensation
I get around people
drives my rational mind insane-
or what's left of my rational mind.
Right now it is shriveled up,
lying somewhere- dead.

How can someone simply change
from dead on their feet
to happy in an instant?
Perhaps they don't.

Death doesn't generate happiness.
But it may bring us numbness.
And, after all, isn't that
what we were searching for?

Everyone Else Is Crazy

You say to me,
The time is come,
it's sad to say;
just you and me now.
We have to stick together-
it's a good thing
you're with me
and I'm with you.
Everyone else is crazy.
We can trust each other,
but don't listen to those
spirits over there.

I tell you,
I love the way you watch;
you don't sway your eyes.
On guard and strong,
always ready to go again.
You make it a new start;
not one of them sees me.
I can say that "friend"
doesn't make a name
the soul of yours.
Again, I tell you-
hear me speaking!
Just you and me now,
for it's everyone else who's crazy.

You tell me,
Don't get caught,
and made to think
this you know
has passed away,
that this you've
always done
keeps you down and down
sifting through my grasp.
Made to think
this here world
is your end to be,
forever fallen
without the likes of me.

I say to you,
Your company keeps me,
so I can sing that song
of calico roan.
I've never doubted your love
or questioned your leading,
or kept you a dark
motion in my past.
It's a good thing I have you,
to raise me up
like the wingless cloud
in it, depthless,
never to hold me down.
I must tell you *again,*
hear me speak!
Don't be made to think

this here world
is your end to be.

You say to me,
There's never a time
to see this now
than that time now
when it has saved you,
I see you grow,
with this, you learn
all I've told you:
have in your soul,
and depart from me please.
I hurt your sight,
for it is our life
we've spent that goes.
To learn a grave,
terrible truth I hold.
You know it is true,
we've hidden it all.
Tell them all
my faithful reason,
I have not let you go.
it is I who only has you.

I tell you,
Not having to fret
us being let loose.
It is why we never dwelt
in any recognized place.
I took you always,
holding you and not caring,
as I say *one last time*,
don't sway your eyes,
and *hear me*!
All that I've told you:
have in your soul,
and depart from me.

And if I never was clear,
I say to you a third time-
you can trust me;
everyone *else* is crazy.

Kristin Baker

The Art of Patience

All who come for you
do since they hold
strength on you
and their fiery judgment.

When the infant cries,
you come to it
or leave just as you came.

When the little girl whimpers,
you must do nothing,
as you know not when she does.

When the father fell,
none often can raise him up,
for he is too strong;
there is nothing to do.

For when a wise man weeps,
it is the most passionate thing;
others watch, unable themselves.

When the dead sleep,
we will sleep.
Come to that,
you could never share;
you do not sleep yet,
therefore you may not
touch the dead
where they lie,
in their soft velvet
'til we come for them.

Kristin Baker

Silent

The empty hollows
inside this heart
are filled
with black,
thick,
dripping,
vile water
that pumps throughout
these veins.
It hurts the heart
until it is molded
into rock that burns
through to this chest.
Only when I have become silent
will this rotting voice
ring out with colorless anger
that turns this face blue,
the face that none have seen.
The one I do not know.
The corrupt will shatter,
plummeting toward solid ground,
which heaves in effort.
All who see will be blinded.
The mere remembrance
will have been banished.

And purity
in this glorious,
bright voice
will have faded.
Disappointment is a gift
that others take pleasure upon.
And those who will object
won't matter at all.

Kristin Baker

A Flower Pointing Down

There is a candle that lights
the ceiling and the floor.
There are eyes
that do not see.

There is a voice that speaks
but is not heard.
There are one million lies
and one million possibilities.

There is a man
who has no one
and a man who needs no one.
There is a man who has someone
and shouldn't.

There are waterfalls
that never end,
and empty souls that want to,
and immortals who are dying
who couldn't.

There is a place where songs
need no voices,
and places where music
is never uttered.

There is a place where lies
set freedom for those
who do not fear the saints,
and wanderers always vanish
when they fall asleep.

Where silence meets
with sweet victory
and notorious troubles are tested,
and make for a remorseful nightfall
and a flower that points down.

Diamond Poem

Risk
your freedom,
a vulnerability.
You are too desperate
to waste time facing your fears.
Now cast away all reality.
Trample on mortality
and take me away
farther.

2. I Had a Name

In the end, what you
Fought so hard not to see
Will become you,
And blind you.

Down

Down, and it goes,
farther than the sweetness of rain
can touch, the light in
our flight that makes it harder
than these wings of flying trees,
and their roots
may keep them from ever departing.
Down is one, who cannot find his breath,
and loses his sight.
We may never know whether
a man is pleased by an inner thought,
or what he has surely seen.
We have never known
if a man fears what it takes
to fight, foreknowing he,
being blind, will not win-
or if he is fearless.
We could never find
that if a man commits a lie,
how it told us who he is.
Down has taken my own lips
parted with corrupt emotions
that take place within the body.
The placement of wings on the body
tells us the day we shall begin to see.
They are there, and what is there:
down, it goes, a lie of life.

Darkening

When you call upon your servant
does he not answer?
The way of happiness occurs
in only the most abstract of places,
as you fade deeper into the emptiness
with no relief of breath.
Joy becomes harder to gather
with the company of others.
It is within arm's grasp, but fear stands between the two.
Loneliness stands to thicken the fear.
And pride can weave together,
forming all your dark thoughts,
taking captive for itself your darkest feelings.
And feeding them back to you.
It is forced upon you in a gluttonous quantity.
Masks hide its treachery as pleasure,
so things that sound simple are never questioned.
Only to bring you blame and regret, your true colors.
Reminds you of all your
failed attempts to hide those fears;
and all those deals stricken with ice cold memories,
stricken with the past.
You call upon it, beginning to darken yourself,
thus revealing to you another side,
hopeless of ever turning back.

My Words, Reformed

Nothing happened. I never should have spoken.
I never should have opened my mouth.
I should have known better.
Every time I do, there's something else
speaking at the same time I am.
It is louder and somehow people hear them, and not me.
And my words are reformed.
It frightens me with how much authority it holds,
threatening to spill my dark secrets, and fears, and backfiring,
always there, and remembering everything, perhaps
in a different way even.
It never changes. I never change.
They don't hear what I am really saying.
I never should have opened my mouth. I thought I knew better.
This is my voice when my mind can't catch up.
It won't listen to my eyes who see unbiasedly.
It takes not into account the things I hear.
It stands alone, fighting against me, reforming what I can't ever say.

The Lion

His strength is beyond what I know.
The power, a different thing entirely.
The words he knows; who he talks to.
He speaks; I try to answer.
But I could never reach his high,
the places he's been, the people he met.
And he speaks; I see his age.
He speaks, but he does not need to tell me this.
I see those crevices rippling the skin
in all the creases that have moved.
The laws he sets are foreign, I have not yet heard them.
Shock strikes their eyes and they flinch back,
only to mourn and yet not repent,
having seen the lion speak but they never heard.

Come Back

Leave.
Come back.
Leave.
Come back.

I have a name.
I have a face.
Please don't
look at my face.
I pray no one
says my name.

I have no age.
I am not younger.
I am no older.
I am just here now.

I leave.
I come back.
I leave.
I come back.

I only have
a face and a name.
No one says my name.
No one sees my face.

Because I come back
and leave again
just to come back.

Kristin Baker

Starry Knights of Day

Toward the short ending in our days of waiting
most will be lost.
All lies and love will mean the same.
Just as chilling air, too rough on the simple skin.
Quick drafts of ice flow in, the doors are locked as they are opened.
And the brilliant sun leading our summer days
open with restless gentle eyes.
A sweet taste per tear on the lacing of blue painted clouds
that has no chance of competition.
The sun has shown our naked truths, shown to her
just when they think she holds high her mountainous stance
who breaths in the sky to care about the insignificant mutterings.
No matter the day, for shadows do not cover her
and the moon does not push her
like the waves that also bow to her.
Fearless light shows a bright reflection to say it knows her queen.
It falters for only this sun to hurtle down from her throne,
her perch of mighty exaltation since her very own creation
in the hands of Him who lets back now
watching her slip.
She falls not alone, but with her lost knights streaking beside her.
They go nowhere but down.
Her moon shall let out his light unable to hold onto her.
It tilts on no axis in no real place.
And they that live are the only ones
who suffer fear and shudder, knowing why, and tilting too.
Having no one to call to whose name is gone.
The starry heaven with which we can see now in the dark day,
too soon, too soon is all that I see.

My moon gave out its light. His queen took my life.

Those knights gone in whispers of the wind that follow them.

And that there are none in refuge to feel fear

until my Lord takes hold of me once again-

only then, my starry knights,

it will be coming surely.

Kristin Baker

Seirafayorla

Coming from the likes of me could this satirical statement depress you so. Your mind has not gone to waste, but what you have been told makes you render your thought to mean nothing. The importance of giving charitably is not their intent but what you blindly believe.

I am not dead to the world, for the world is dead to me, and what we contribute also holds no value or importance. This new feeling is but a pretty sound we hear and love irrevocably. And the serenity it gives us has shown us comfort that we need, when we do not fight for our minds but let them go with the storm clouds that give us nothing in return.

Now sleep late into the day, child; the bruises in your eyes have blended but stayed. When your dreams have withered away, your life will remain as silent as an immovable object.

You seek help that does not come, and so it fails as a necessity after a time. The frightening dream becomes enjoyable. For years we have said it is not important enough to worry about now. Nothing comes to help us or live a life with us. I wake up crying, but I am safe within my given angel's arms, and though I am not silent, my words are never heard. And they say that I will fly away from this home someday, and this Seirafayorla will leave me.

I don't know why I love her, but I do, and I need her like a lifeline. She tells me to let go, but I do not. I listen to what she says, for I love her, but it is irrelevant if I love her feeling nothing, and so I am never heard. This here angel is unsmiling, like a shadow too far from my reach and a trumpet too far to hear completely.

My mind has gone to waste but not yours, child. I see because that was what I was looking for. We are only opposites who drifted away from each other. A grave shadow, harmless beneath my eyes. My angel, strange as she seems to be, raises me no higher, and a lie does not pass through her vacant tongue. She is a conscience to see back on when memory falters, and I need such thing.

She sees me when I don't see. When I sleep, my face is a shadow, and I am nothing more than just a cool, grim memory. My angel sings, just a trumpet, too far to hear completely. The fragments I only hear, sweet Seirafayorla that she belongs far from my reach, and her song lies in my stars when I sleep. To dream of the sleeping stars is no less than what I want. And she, that sings, sounding far off, calls the stars, and then do I dream to the patter of a coming lullaby that is yet to be needed.

To Say Good-Bye

This is not good-bye for I will you;

come back in more than a memory,

noticeable as thunder and strong as lightning.

However, if you do come back as just a memory,

you will be remembered as obviously as a hint of thunder,

and your remaining love as powerful

as the strike of light.

For changing only means the people you know

become people you knew.

The difference between pain and remembering will be thin.

My Name Sang to Itself

Your name shall not identify you.
It is not your title.
It is not your home.
It is not your life.
I once had a name
so beautiful
it sang to itself.
So quietly, so softly, so deep.
So kind, so shamelessly and envied.
But now I hold humility
close to me.
I dwell here in the dirt.
And my name does not define me.
It does not know me.
It won't feed me.
I have no name
to live on.
And my name is gone away.
Gone like the shadows
who never dwell.
I once had a name.
It sang to itself.
So quietly, so softly, so deep.

Discolored

I am discolored and wobbly.
sitting on stilts,
though I am sleeping
under a still moon.
My stance is faulty.
I topple over,
my weight with me.
a troublesome curse,
a silent, cold memory,
distant in my head,
tortures me
'til I scream.
My colors
on my sleeve-
what I am-
discolored.

Immortal Fire

The lesser of these two flames
when one burns even brighter
and white as the snowy hair atop my head,
is my fire of eternity as long as I have been burning.
It is these hell bearers
behind human flesh- they proclaim-
who smoke me.
There is nothing left for them to smoke,
I put out all of their fires
long ago when my flame here it began to flicker,
until I started to burn.
And that which fear has stricken upon me as lightning,
cursing my fiery heart into an electric frenzy,
spiraling and clutching this
that cannot reach the stars to reach reality
is only a distant vision of white.
The land of hell bearers where my people burned and died
left me the last to burn bright sparks of tears
and immortal fire.

What Kills Me

There is something inside me
in a place in my heart
where no person will ever go.
A place underneath the
many unimportant things.
It shines brighter than light.
It is warm,
makes me burn,
lets me go another day,
lets me trust.
It is something I do not know.
It is something I do not want to know.
It is sweet,
and it plays a beautiful melody.
It is stunning,
and makes other things stunning.
It sings my heart to sleep, and I dream.
I will sleep forever . . .

Body vs. Mind

My body and mind
are so disconnected,
I do things without knowing.
I am still when I'm in pain,
and I toss in my sleep.
When I think things that sound right,
my voice misinterprets.
I am not scared, yet small things
make me jump up ten feet in the air.
I see things that aren't there.
I talk for hours to no one.
My mind has a reality
no one else seems to see.
And I know I'll die in my dreams.

Means to Be

What it means to be Responsible is
you have to be an adult
before you can start being a kid.
What it means to feel Loved is
you have to see the brighter side
of every gloomy shadow.
What it means to be Smart is
you can't rely on your own mind
to see every perspective of things.
What it means to be Patient is
you have to accept the things
that are the most difficult to understand.
What it means to be Respected is
you have to acquire no enemies
in your most depressing days.
What it means to be Humble is
you have to step before the lowest
and see the side of pain.
What it means to be Courageous is
you step between the stranger and the sword
and beg it to choose you instead.
What it means to be Merciful is
you have to forgive the unforgivable
and attract them with your sweet tongue.

What it means to be Aware is
you have to reach beneath the surface
and scour the land for its deeper meaning.
What it means to be Available is
you have to feel their pain
and prepare yourself for the end.
The mind is limitless
you must protect it with your life.

The Distraction

The streets of the city are black tonight.
There is a timeless sense in the street lamps
as the critters fog up the glow who fly about,
as travelers who make it to summit of Everest.
There is a glassy layer of mist on the asphalt boulevard.
Every car coming towards me, and passes me,
shooting me with their light beams
also glisten off the charcoal mirror.
I write this, and find the possibility that I
can find more than the travelling lights
like a dream, they open a doorway.
And to where my heart beats the loudest
I, too can be found there or my own path.
My footprints leave a trail
beside the doorway.

Last Memories

The bird croaks and the frog flies.

The stars falter from an assault.

The cat has kissed the shaking foe.

And the leaves have mourned for their coming leader.

They all shiver while they wait.

The water has poisoned its consumers.

And the sun tripped over its fallen stars.

All who've come have cried, and those who stayed have died.

Toxic gases have pleased thieves and wanderers.

The babe who could fly far enough,

struggling to stay up, glanced back

at what death the light brought to them all,

that had given him mercy,

and it still was not enough.

After-Death

Through the foggy days which peer up to me,
down under, where they see
all things are going about them.
In time, those restful, grave eyes,
who look upon many, yet understand none.
I joined them, as did all;
I joined them first.
As I look up through
the foggy days, in restful eyes,
who peer silently at all in wonder,
I am dead as the soil I join.
Those I see tread falls of silver,
yet never to pride or frightful vengeance
when fault lies on none, but go on to learn-
by where I stepped, before I left-
where they might be going.
All will attend indifferently,
if not the thought, that I may see them.
They cannot hear me, but my blood treads
beneath their footsteps,
not giving, but watching,
seeing how they treat me when I am gone.
How they treat my dwelling of nothing . . .
And everything.

Blind Vulture

The feeling is mutual.
Your blind perceptions
into the hearts of all that you know-
if you had not been so lucky,
they would rip you into pieces.
In your garment of blessed blood-dwelling skin.
Remembering the fear that rips me apart
gives away every soul.
You blind me with this taste, and this hold that I love.
I do not see any more a reason that you care.
What strikes more than pain, as these walls close in on me,
is this, that I have been cut.
Only when I rip myself apart,
will I seek revenge,
and cast out these demons
as that which only I loved,
is shattered, blood cold, by the spirit.

Midnight Turns to Dawn

To Ms. Wilson

As the midnight turns to dawn,
my mind instinctively searches for the light
in a charcoal black that lasts-
where darkness no longer grows.
And as the ritual of the oldest sun's rays
suddenly become the shine of morning,
a deep veil
that once had no control,
and had its limits,
reveals only that death's plan
finally tells its story.

As dawn turns to dusk,
irony plays into a treason
in which destiny
wins over all of its children,
while the curse is their master.
They see the sun,
and the shadows whisper threats
but take no soul.
It was just a dream.
Reality dawns upon death's children,
and they feel
not only the enduring rain,
but the chilling breath of the water.

And dawn and dusk become overturned
their purposes are rendered meaningless.
The end of the rain never comes,
but midnight fills the air,
swallowing up our children.

As dusk turns to midnight,
it's so wet that you cannot see
a difference between the salty seas
and acid waters descending from stars.
The sun can only rise
into a gloomy era,
as black as night.
Things are seen only with the eyes,
and not felt with the heart-
as legend tells.
It is too cold to notice the sun's rays,
the children of the sun,
and endure the comfort
that sweeps the clouds far north
where the chill is left behind,
along with the children of death.
 . . . We are the children of death

Kristin Baker

When I Walk

As I walk, behind me there is not a shadow
that will dare to walk with me into my demise.
Who am I to bear the sweet shade of gray?
I try to see, yet I am nothing but a traveling blind man,
having a path set for me by the stars I cannot see.
When I walk, I am no less than a weak shadow.
I hold no grip on reality, or control of my path.
I seek not a destination, but a sense,
whereas I am arrived with no purpose,
and those who look
see nothing in me but a shoe with no host,
or that nothing is set within my soul.
I look through the mirror,
to see that as of midnight,
I had asked of me, what I am but late,
and would ask that the door remain open,
a door to receive me and lead me home.
Yet who am I, being unprepared and hollow.
Who am I to have a refuge, an ending?
Lest I had come, and beheld
that the door was shut!

A Dance with a Beat

I move my sturdy hips,
roll them around like they
don't belong to me.
My hair is a bouquet
delicately designed
where the leaves sway
in every direction.
My feet swivel and turn
to spin my body.
I lift my arms to the air
like they're floating away,
finally drifting apart
like opposites of magnets,
easing more on each side
outstretched for none,
given room to fly and run
slide, reach, twirl, and turn.
All I have as excess is gone
living in a body of water in my mind,
leaving me just with this
body of a cat
on its two back feet,
running and jumping
and whirling and curling.

Curling just as a ball
before it makes its approach,
the final big entrance
announcing its song.
I dance for a tune,
a soundless tune.
One with a rhythm-
with no rhyme so far.
One with an echo
that comes from my heart.
One with a beat
that once lit the stars.

Follow My Wings

Follow my wings,
you can't see my face.
Every reason tells you
I am no good.
My blood is white.
I am pure.
I'll lead you
where nothing hurts.
The road you travel
is purposeless.
Just follow my wings.
Your mind is corrupt
and you find no peace
in those you meet.
I can love you,
teach you the truth,
give you comfort and warmth
if you follow my horns.
Whatever you want
is deceitful here.
It is dark.
So look for my beady eyes.
I'll lead you to light.

You have no bonds,
no burdens or tasks.
Your job is finished.
Let me be for you.
I'll lead you right.
Take my hand
and watch my wings
intertwine
and watch my body
shine.
Follow my voice.

3. Change is Coming

Poetry cannot be written,
But only sung.
Not designed, but easy coming.
Not a symbol, but a taste.

Invisible

Room one,
there is yelling.
It can be logical
or ridiculous.
I step forward
into the light.
This does not
concern me.

Room two,
someone is leaving.
No, several are going.
My opinion is not
relevant for here.
What can *I* do?

Room three,
who is this?
Can I get out
fast enough?
They all stare at me.
Am I doing
something wrong?

Room four,
dark and quiet,
separate from all else.
I stay because it
is not confusing
to choose to be here.
I stay because
I am invisible.
Here, I cast no shadow.
Here, I am no burden.
Here, they cannot see me.
And here, I cannot see me.

Kristin Baker

Morning Walk

Morn, we know it   has to come,

like it does   bring each day

whether it was   being the choice

of hand to go.   The dirt is felt,

and grass is dry.   May I

rather walk   without my shoes?

Eastern sunrise,   lakeside view,

all of my   past thoughts

drifting in   the ocean

and landing ashore

on a different   country far-off.

These dreams   I have given up.

Midday comes-   none hear me say

I am different   because I

do not stay.   Those worries

in my reach   I haven't feared

for someone else   watches me,

has my thoughts.   Even breaks

so suddenly   with a hard snap.

First colors in blue

gray, orange, pink,   purple, and red

before the   glimpse of dark.

These colors   sing to me.

The day between   two days

still and hollow   beckons no light,

finding comfort   in a word.

Let no day   come again,

but until   the sunrise,

there are   no laws

we could have ever broken.

Land of Gray Clouds

The time of change has come.
The leaves have spread out
on the dusty gravel,
reaching like the arms of fire,
and devouring their host.
And the clouds, wrapped in truth,
leave trails lightly throughout the pastures
where God's tranquil whispers
can wash away
your fear of blood.
The chiming falls of the water's last pass,
are as sweet silver tears.
May the land rise again
and hail the sky,
and all its mysteries.
Where day and night falter where their sins
have been discovered,
captured and taken away
from the land of clouds-
our protectors.
And might the fear
be brushed from my skin
by the angel's wings,
leaving no more
than the highest expectations.
Oh, the land of gray clouds!

The Irrelevant Song

Each day is a cloudy day.
the air is cool, misty;
the wind gently cradles my face.
The invisible air bathes me in silk-
velvet when I look up.
I hide behind the clouds.
The future is always foggy,
and the sky is hidden,
with everything else.
I can hear music
from the ground nearby.
I can see bright blue music-
it sings for me,
not in exchange for anything.
The song is no where
in soft words that comfort me,
in my cloudy day, cradling me.
A sweet song is in my arms.
Each new line
builds to the climax
where there is none in the icy winds;
a border line in the clouds.
I shall sing a song,
sweetened by the hidden sun;
the fire in my throat.

Rain beats down
when my hands are raised,
and I cry; it stings my eyes.
In the arms of the angel,
the song will never end,
and the clouds will remain.
We stay when the night comes,
and our song is irrelevant,
and we sing.
The rain sings back to us
in return.
And when we raise our hands in hope,
I hold up my angel, protected . . .

Kristin Baker

Rain Lullaby

Wash me over with clouds
and tuck me in with a deep
comfortable sense of darkness.
Sing me to sleep with the patter of rain,
the crackling of brilliant lightning,
and the soothing beat
of the restless thunder
whispering to me,
"Once more,
this night holds for you."
And the stars beneath my feet,
the world above my reach!

Land of the Dead

For my mother

They asked me to
recall a day from my past.
I chose the day I finally heard you laugh.
It was a day when not a single man died,
a day a lie was not uttered,
and there was not a blemish in the sky.
I visited the Land of the Dead.
I saw there beautiful children wearing black.
And I saw their blank expressions,
as they did not feel pain.
And could not remember what it was like.
A little girl, she was stunning;
she said her name was Lila Reilee.
Her steady, lithe stance and auburn eyes
were piercing as she looked at me, puzzled.
Still, she was not fully there with me;
she was still back,
back in the place of change
where it was too quiet for the winds to move.
Here in the Land of the Dead,
they whispered to me sweet hymns
and all the things that had been done.
It was the beautiful autumn day,
the day I heard you laugh.

Oh, how musical it was-
so serene and flawless,
without a care in the world.
And yet . . . maybe it was only
an echo of your cry.

A Friend

A friend is someone
who cares enough to get in your face
if you're doing something stupid.
They'd stick up for you no matter the cost
and would humiliate you
just because you ask for it!
They will stay up with you
until six in the morning,
talking on the phone if you need them.
They will be as crazy as you are,
and forgive you for being just plain retarded.
They don't lie to you,
steal from you,
or become angry with you for something small.
They'll tell you if you're being a pain in the ass,
rude, or just being annoying.
They'd look after you
if you were temporarily incapable.
They won't ignore you, or make you cry,
unless you really needed it.
They can even make you laugh
when you cry.
They'll talk with you,
if you have a secret,
or about anything you wouldn't
trust anyone else with.
They'll allow you to be yourself,
and will only occasionally be embarrassed
about being your friend.
But they won't judge you . . .

One Million Lies, One Million Possibilities

I'm not lost.

I can't do this anymore.

Love and forgiveness counteract.

I'll be on time.

There's no such thing as sad.

It's not as bad as it seems.

There's still time.

I was lying.

I miss you.

I'm fine.

There'll be someone.

I didn't mean it.

You can do it.

No one wants to hear it.

I'll be there.

I understand.

It's not what it looks like.

Emotions are healthy.

No one will find out.

I don't know what you're talking about.

I hate you.

Lying is hard.

I cannot be influenced.

My mind is safe.

You'll get better.

I don't know.

I'm content.

Loving is easy.

I'm not loved.

Everybody lies.
It hurts too much.
It's not important.
I don't care.
I'm almost done.
Misery loves company.
I hate myself.
Well, if that's what you want . . .
I'm not a kid anymore.
I always felt the same.
I didn't do it.
It takes time.
I don't know who I am.
I love you.

A picture can make a thousand words,
and one word can mean ten thousand things.

Kristin Baker

Night Sky

In the night sky
there are many leaves
and darkened mountains
and shouting, brilliant stars
that sing when played in a tune.
But the mountains aren't free enough.
They stay for music to ring from their tops.
the trees bristle, giving way for those more sturdy,
rooted into their lakes, searching for any light miles away,
waiting for some kind of life to come for them soon,
declaring love to the fallen limbs' dancing feet
that find no love too soon; hope fading
when the trumpets and bells cease.
A drifting stream softly flows by,
mixing them with sweet colors
of their poignant tears,
tempted by wind.

Move

They never say live a full life,
but only live your life.
They crucify you for not living it
the way they want, and therefore,
you are truly not allowed to live.
You remain stuck in the same place,
not changing, or fearing it.
But a change is surely coming, carelessly, yet
just as bike chains loosen
when no support comes to show.
Yes, the change is coming,
and the moving aside of those
who stand in the way of it.
But you have no height,
your eyes hold no depth,
and therefore are gray as flat paint.
The ability to die or understand mortality
gives you a right to live, they say.
Then what you do
and who you then chose to be
shine as glistening eyes
toward the sturdy ground you seek,
and the path you make.
Surrounded by beautifully fake, immortal flowers
who cannot themselves walk the path,
are those who had to change, but didn't,
are those who could not stay the same, they were told,
and refused to follow, despite it all,
are those who appear . . .
scentless.

Grass

There is no difference in grass;
none are older,
none are younger.
They are all children,
growing and playing,
dancing and laughing,
gathering up the leaves,
cuddling with the raindrops,
living next to the bugs
(who are called "lady"
but act like children),
surrendering to the
evil creatures that
take their lives
(over and over),
brushing alongside
each other's backs,
letting them know
they will protect them.
They are all children.

Graceful wanderer

Nomad to the pleasant winds

Moon tides guide you now

Love Is

The war that never ends,
where both sides still wake each day
ten times as willing to fight it
than the day before.

Love is . . .
Seeing another's pain
and instead of feeling mutual pain,
you tend to their needs over desires.

Love is . . .
Staring death in the eye,
watching it advance,
and yet being unafraid.
For you can see everything else.

Love is . . .
Knowing the outcome,
seeing the consequences,
and feeling victorious.

Love is . . .
Not a thing done by a person
but a thing that people only have
the honor of being included in.

Love is . . .
An existence by the will of God.
He is love.

Love is . . .
Seeing all perspectives
and not being able to conceive the thought
that yours is most important.

Love is . . .
Not something that can only be done
by bloodline,
by labor,
by devotion,
by happiness,
or by force.
Love is . . .
Everywhere and inside anyone.

Love is . . .
Willing to do something
rather than simply
wanting to or needing to.

Love is . . .
Blindly falling
and still somehow knowing
exactly where you're going.

Kristin Baker

Love is . . .
The meaning most people don't see
because they're too busy looking
at the smaller things.

Love is . . .
Not the absence of hate
but the presence of a different kind of warmth.

Love is . . .
The only warmth left
after the last friend has gone.

Love is . . .
Not pride
but something to be proud of.

Love is . . .
Not being in the right direction
but bringing others to the right direction.

Love is . . .
The root of all evil
when Spirit leaves the world.
Those who chose never lose it.
It's not easy to ignore,
and God never leaves us.

Love is . . .
The indestructible,
the fearless,
the merciful,
the thought,
the peacemaker of all hate.

Love is . . .
The immortal.

I can't know what love truly is.
I am too young to know.
so I am full of doubt . . .
but love . . .

Love is . . .
Not wrong.
And love . . .

Love is . . . doubtless.

Kristin Baker

He Is Coming

Is he coming?
Say the greatest
of the highest gazing peaks.
Is he near?
Cry the gentle birds,
disguises of the roaming spirits
aiming for the heavens.
Do you see him?
Wonder passing cubs and pups.
Is it a sign?
Scream the green full trees,
swaying and clapping their hands.
I do hope so,
Sighs the tallest of them all.
A chocolate furry chipmunk
nestled in its perch.
Can you hear it?
Ask the vibrant lively lights
that reach up toward forever
whenever darkness clouds their sight.
And share the music they catch.
Have you felt it?
Is he coming?
Do you see him?
Am I late?
It hurts your heart to wonder . . .
All these things who cry to Him who raises
were invited to His gates.

Explanation

What you think I write,
I write
when you worry
what I write.
We think the same way,
just don't see the same way.
And heavens of hell
in lies caused by grief,
thinking what I write
leaves no space for assuming.
Saying what I mean? . . .
Oh, that's just cruel!
Between two lines
is another line.
This line is a thought of mine;
what I saw as I wrote.
Nothing good-
good, I hope.
And the minute you start to think
you've found me
and where I am,
you've found my thought;
for it's all why I stand.
And all you see is me.
But hear me whisper this line-
there, you will see love.
"I am not love,
but love is in me."

No Bonds

Can I go with you
little graceful wanderer,
and no bonds hold us?

Your feathers, so smooth.
So many different colors-
all you do is fly.

Fly over oceans-
beneath dark skies of gray clouds
lies your destiny.

Skim the cool rivers-
your reflection an angel,
who then leaves again.

The water carries
your reflection down the stream,
and you go farther.

Take me, Wanderer,
go past the places you've been-
see all that you see.

My own reflection,
when this time comes to an end,
always beside yours.

And the dark waters,
looking up at the gray skies-
our time never ends.

River

I am a stone.
My sides are rigid and cracked,
discolored and black.
The river people come and clean me,
pick me up, smooth out edges.
I am white and lovely.
And the river people
set me back
beside the river
to watch it fill the valleys
and lap up at the shore,
tossing diamonds against the sand,
where I live;
where the river people come,
come and feel my cracks
and caress my wounded feet.

Name

I do not know my own name.
Mother Rain stole my precious title.
I told her I was in love with her child,
little baby Bow,
and Old Mother Rain cast me away,
away, away, away from my lover.
She shouts a storm of threats
and now she has stolen my name!
Oh, I search in Mr. Pond.
Who turns purple at Lord Sun's command,
where messy muck traps itself for all eternity.
So I search the Trickling Creek-
oh lovely nomad, you travel,
who carries little life on your back.
How I search Lady River's swarming cadets-
long and hard they work,
protecting River's home.
For without my name,
how shall I wed my beloved Bow?
Oh, how I'll swim the mighty seas for him!

The Mountain

Of the winds on the mountain,
in the higher of the peaks,
every breath it takes
of the roaring tides
at a point blank fall
down the end.

An expression in places
you never knew felt,
as it cuts each movement
leaking through a light
on a ridge.

Where the end leads upward,
and even faltered raging wind,
is when I do
hear its silence.

For the waves there below
are just fragments of here,
and a face I see
that rests on the ridge holding light
is when it gives color
to the mountain.

Here I stand.
And . . . here I listen.
And . . . here I wait.

Traveling Car

Wherever I go

I spit and grumble and screech

I am hot and I sweat, I sweat, I sweat

I don't slow down easy

and my sides are shattered, are shattered, are shattered.

I haven't been used in a while,

but when I am, I am, I am,

we go yonder to beautiful places.

The ground I roll on is black and silky smooth, silky smooth, silky smooth.

I enjoy where I go.

The cool mist splashes upon my face, my face, my face.

I may be old and worn

and my insides are searing, searing, searing.

My feet may be blistered and torn,

and I sometimes don't see where I am going.

But better places lay yonder, and yonder, and yonder

when I travel-

and the roads may occasionally hurt my feet.

But the distance I travel, I travel, I travel

is greatly rewarded,

and we are changing, changing, changing . . .

Felt Like Rain

There was a time, but only a moment,
when you could be blatant but clever.
it was when the winds were still,
trying not to stir the dances of mirrors,
reflecting what we do not see for ourselves;
reflecting the hidden.
The skies were gray, and the darkening clouds
of late noon were the same as midnight.
And it felt like rain.

No snow or hail- where a hulking cloud drifting so low
can only give a glimpse as to what would come.
They all wanted to dance and play,
and laugh in a bed of green.
So you could not deny a sense of love,
and you felt like rain.

It does not spray, or mist, or sprinkle
like on the grass in summer. But came down on us.
Nothing else worth waking up to,
or staying inside for, or drifting to sleep in.
The creatures will hide below in their cover,
while the birds in the sky find shade from the showers.
Nothing else worth listening to,
in the dark, in the warmth.
Where nothing outside holds shelter,
but ends up as extra showers
when we have nothing else to do,
and we felt like rain.

There truly is no darkness,
no separation of language;
all of it is just a dream. Not a bad dream,
but still dark and we can see, we see lights,
mountains, fields, rain, and music.
But there are no people, or the moon,
or machines, or time,
for they are a part of the dream.
No thirst, or words, or hate.
Because it felt like rain.

There are the earth people.
Their salty tears melt into the acidic drops.
Their coats are blackened water,
but it is good. No other description.
They are not deceived, and they adore the rain.
It tells them stories, and they are never forgotten.
And they felt like rain.

Kristin Baker

I try to forget the things I see in their faces,

sitting amongst the dampened grass with the sweet scent,

lighting me in flames,

then putting me out when I lay back.

There is no one else, and I roll around and laugh awhile.

No weight of the world holds me, yet I see the clouds.

They are not harmful, and I am not cold.

No worries, or fears, or grief, or pain,

or lonesomeness, or time.

The sky never ends in the east or the west,

or the north or the south.

Nothing comes up to me and bothers me

because I can't be bothered.

I am dreaming and I am sleeping,

and I slept awhile,

because I felt like rain.

Then there was a time, but only a moment,

when you could be blatant but clever.

It was when the winds were still,

trying not to stir the dances of mirrors,

reflecting what we do not see for ourselves;

reflecting the hidden.

The skies were gray, and the darkening clouds

of late noon were the same as midnight.

And then there was rain.